WISE FROM WITHIN

WISE FROM WITHIN

Jo Giordano

WISE FROM WITHIN

iUniverse books may be ordered through booksellers or by contacting:

iUniverse
1663 Liberty Drive
Bloomington, IN 47403
www.iuniverse.com
844-349-9409

Because of the dynamic nature of the Internet, any web addresses or links contained in this book may have changed since publication and may no longer be valid. The views expressed in this work are solely those of the author and do not necessarily reflect the views of the publisher, and the publisher hereby disclaims any responsibility for them.

Any people depicted in stock imagery provided by Getty Images are models, and such images are being used for illustrative purposes only. Certain stock imagery © Getty Images.

ISBN: 978-1-6632-0645-9 (sc)
ISBN: 978-1-6632-1516-1 (hc)
ISBN: 978-1-6632-0644-2 (e)

Library of Congress Control Number: 2020914428

Print information available on the last page.

iUniverse rev. date: 12/14/2020

The daily morning announcement scripts are designed to be read every day by the oldest students in the school over the loud speaker. Afterwards, students or teachers in the smaller classroom can re-read the message and unpack the content if time allows. The day-by-day tradition creates a routine and serves as a building block for personal development.

Start the day with intention. Words are powerful.

Repetition works. Create your wise from within.

How to Use this Book

1) Distribute to school leaders.

2) Choose team for reading morning announcements over the loud speaker of the school: 4 or 5 of the students from the oldest grade, with a commitment to leadership, who would benefit from public speaking practice.

3) Connect team with 1 adult mentor to assist with daily preparation. Independence, if desired, may be attained after approximately 3 months of coaching.

4) Assign each student to the same section of the script. Students know their zone and have their own book to prepare at home.

5) Rehearse as team 5 -10 minutes before going live on morning announcements. Pay attention to slow delivery, clear communication, and tone of voice.

6) Repeat. This book provides scripts for half of a school year. Once completed, or a large break in the school calendar has been reached, repeat from beginning page to start the renewal of the school year.

Alternative Uses:

- Individual classrooms use separately.

- Families use to start the day.

~ From my desk to yours ~
I hope this book serves your school the way it has mine. That's the gift of teaching: to serve. I have been teaching Physical Education at a K-8 school in Asheville, NC since 2003. I am a proud teacher and life-long learner. Kids are my tribe. After earning my Masters in P.E. I launched into my self-prescribed "School of Life" degree. I became a wanna-be neuroscientist and an aspiring liaison for holistic education.
There have been times in my life, especially when reading inspirational texts, when I have thought: "Why didn't they teach me that in school?" I began to realize they probably tried, but it wasn't repeated enough. I now understand how repetition wires pathways in our mind. When I began incorporating brain science and self-care science into my classes, I kept hearing from parents that they wished they had these lessons growing up. I expanded to the school's morning announcements. Similarly, my fellow teachers and administrators enjoyed the reminders to start the school day with a nod to social and emotional learning. Here is a ready-made morning announcement book for you. Play hard, live easy.
Jo Giordano

Foreword

What we think, we become. What we feel, we attract. What we imagine, we create. Through daily practice, we can build and strengthen the pathways to our greatest self. Master your morning. Speak your daily script.

The subconscious mind is forming when we are young. Later in life, we realize how important this massive memory bank is to our happiness and joyful experience. We make most of our big life decisions based on that inner voice, whether we realize it or not. The best way to strengthen the subconscious is through positive and consistent repetition. Are we training the voice in school enough? Do we start the school day with a message that is worth memorizing?

In schools, we can use the morning announcements to repeat the important life lessons and highlight the techniques of how to learn. This book serves as a daily message to energize the most important subjects in education: self-love and self-discovery.

Envision a school day that is rich with confidence, self-care, and vitality. Adults and students remind one another to be in charge of their brain development: a collective force of inspiration. Teachers take breaks to refuel. People arrive to school, gifted the tools of how to learn, and greet the most powerful human computer (the brain) with the respect it deserves. Water, nutrition, sleep patterns, growth mindset, morning routines, gratitude, connection to others, exercise - these lessons are part of the morning greeting. Let's create that school day.

Example Page 1

Speaker 1 reads very
SLOWLY

wise words from an amazing human

person's name

Speaker 2 WAITS for
quote to settle

- - -
- - -
- - -

question to ponder

Speaker 2 reads
SLOWLY

Speaker 3 reads

paragraph 1*

Speaker 4 reads

paragraph 2*

Speaker 5 reads

paragraph 3*

*If there is a list rather than paragraphs, divide up the parts evenly

A good first impression can work wonders.

J.K. Rowling

How do you want to be remembered at this school?

Imagine your principal had a visitor in school today and it turned out to be your biggest hero or icon. Would they remember you from your first impression?

People have studied the science of meet and greets. Most people hear your words, but it isn't what they are focusing on. Here is a short list of characteristics that people notice:
- good eye contact
- confident posture
- the tone of your voice
- body language
- facial gestures
- a calm or excitable manner

Whether you are seeing an old friend or meeting a new teacher, greetings matter. Ask three adults to teach you their lesson on making a good first impression. Live the way you want to be remembered.

Emotion is created by motion.
The more you move, the better you feel.

Tony Robbins

Is your schedule set up so your toughest class subjects are after exercise?

Whatever subjects come directly after exercise will likely be your most successful. These time periods are when your brain synapses are most ready for new information and can lock it into long-term memory.

The prefrontal cortex is awake and ready to learn when it is primed up after big movement. A tired mind simply will not lock in new information.

If you want to spend more time playing and less time studying, don't waste your time with a tired brain in class. You'll just have to relearn the information all over again. Instead, find a way to exercise in between classes and your brain will go from feeling drained to feeling entertained.

Understanding that we
are essentially water is
the key to understanding
the mysteries of
the universe.

Masaru Emoto

Are you drinking enough
water to function like
a champion?

Successful people are not just lucky. They leave little clues that you can follow. A person who is serious about getting ahead in life uses hydration for peak performance.

If you interviewed every Olympic athlete, you would learn that they take hydration seriously and drink water before, during, and after performance. It boosts your mood to feel good, and gets the brain and muscles functioning at the highest level possible.

The best way to feel a major effect of water is to drink a full water bottle in the morning when you first wake up. If you really want to feel good, add some lemon to that water. Throughout the day, drink a bottle of water every 2 hours. The benefits of such a simple daily practice may be the difference between being tired and being inspired.

Play is really the work of childhood.

Mr. Rogers

If you were able to watch yourself play in a game, would you see a happy and fair teammate?

We learn and communicate through play. 5-minute blocks of games in between classes allows us to accomplish more in the day. In general, our brain's attention span lasts for about 10 minutes at a time. Exercise wakes us up.

So how do we focus on tough lessons and keep our brains from getting flooded or drifting? Play "full out" when there are breaks in the day. If your teacher gives you a brain break every 20 minutes, prove you can handle it.

Control your body, volume level, and emotions and you'll likely get rewarded with a boost of endorphins and that head-nodding approval look of an impressed adult. Classrooms that play together, stay together.

The way you start your
day determines how
well you live your day.

Robin Sharma

Can you manage your
morning routine at home?

The majority of top athletes, millionaires, and leaders recommend creating a specific morning routine for yourself. Yet, many people around us claim that they are not morning people. The faster you reformulate that belief, the better.

Studies have found that we can actually reshape our thinking. The part of your brain called the prefrontal cortex is associated with emotions. It's possible to train for happy reactions to getting out of bed and memorizing a healthy routine.

You know what's better than the snooze button? Being in the same club as top athletes and the leaders of the world. So, create a morning ritual, write it down with specific times, and hang it on your wall. It usually takes 66 days for this to become a life-long habit. In a short time you will have a morning manifesto worth millions.

The biggest adventure you can ever take is to live the life of your dreams.

Oprah Winfrey

What is one idea you would like to make come true?

Many inventors throughout history made certain they took time for daydreaming and relaxing their mind each day. They believed that our imagination could lead us to the best ideas for our future.

Some even say we are inventing and shaping our lives with our thought patterns and emotions. If we sit still and paint a picture in our mind, over time, we will begin to see it in reality.

What if each day you gave yourself the time to sit back and imagine your life in the future? You may find the vision to work in your favor. If you're not sure if those inventors were right about the intelligence of fantasy, isn't it worth finding out? We become what we think about most often.

Take the first step in faith. You don't have to see the whole staircase, just take the first step.

Marian Wright Edelman

What if we make things seem more scary in our head?

We do this. We stall on doing things because it is difficult to step out of our comfort zone. That is absolutely normal because it is a function of our brain to keep us safe. It takes courage to work past this feeling.

When you are considering doing something a little uncomfortable, or even downright annoying, your brain immediately begins talking you out of it. In order to bypass that survival part of your brain, you need to start programming it.

Start small with overcoming the trickery of morning laziness. Your mind tells you it's foggy but it's not true. Your brain is the most efficient and creative in the first few hours of the day, if you don't hit the snooze button. The ability to wake up and use that brilliance is step 1 to reprogramming it for an expanded reality.

You are the author of your own story.

Lisa Nichols

If you could play any role in a book, what would it be?

What experience do most lead characters in movies, books, and plays have in common? They are all different people in different stories, but in general, they learn to listen to their own voices and desires.

They usually follow a pattern of struggle and self-discovery. Some people say a main character circles through the stages of a hero's journey. At first they are influenced by what everyone else says, and through time, they find the strength to turn towards their own intelligence.

How does this happen in our own lives? Do we stay distracted by everyone else and miss the chance to check in with our own compass? When we get to watch other peoples' stories, it's fairly easy to give suggestions. What would you tell yourself in order to be the strong lead role in your life? Go forth and find your true north.

Pick a goal that makes
you want to jump out of
bed in the morning.

What if every morning
you woke up and said,
"The entire universe
is on my side"?

Michael Beckwith

Pressing the snooze button is scientifically proven to make people more tired. Your body thinks you are going back into a deep sleep cycle of 90 minutes. When that doesn't happen, you are waking from a disrupted pattern in your brain.

Sleep researchers say that the snooze button takes the brain 2 hours to recover. Normally a person feels groggy and unfocused for 15 minutes after waking. That's called sleep inertia. Snooze makes that stage 5-15 times longer.

When you hit snooze, you lose the trust of your brain. In response, unfortunately, you lose focus, attention, memory and discipline throughout the day. Be straight-up honest with your wake up time, hop out of bed, and your mind will be your biggest fan. Win the morning, win the day.

When you write it, you ignite it.

Joseph McClendon III

Do you know why everyone suggests writing thoughts down on paper?

A major part of having a great memory is writing. The act of slowing down the mind to write facts, goals, and notes from class is much more powerful than we realize. It encodes information as a personal experience. Typing notes often is not enough. Our mind knows it is not *our* information and we often forget it.

When you write with a pen or pencil you ignite the power of participation. Writing notes in your own words tells your brain that you are a partner in the experience. It connects creative and logical sides of your brain. Offer your mind a memory stick of familiar hand-written images, and you'll get a free upgrade.

Rewards come in action, more than in discussion.

Tony Robbins

How will you reward yourself for completing this month of school in style?

The beginning of a new year is a fresh start. You usually have more organization and motivation. Do you want those feelings to last? There is a chemical in our brain that controls our motivation to do something and the reward feeling that comes from accomplishing it: the neurotransmitter is called dopamine. Rewards work.

Some of the chemical signals in our brain make us feel good, confident, and motivated to do more. Dopamine is one of those organic, good chemicals in our brains. If you want to reward yourself for a great first month of school, a solid choice is play and adventure.

Try choosing 3 specific goals to meet, and when accomplished, celebrate with 3 friends for an adventure you've been wanting to do for a while. You'll be training your brain and rewarding the motivation that you want to continue.

The words that come
out of your mouth,
come into your life.

Jen Sincero

When you choose
words to speak about
your life, are they
negative or positive?

There is a very old and common belief that says: What you think, you become. What you feel, you attract. What you imagine, you create. If your common language includes phrases like: I can't, that's not fair, I'm not good at that, I'll never be, and it's just too hard – there is a cloud following you around called fixed mindset.

Studies show that when you begin retraining your words, you are creating pathways in your brain. Your inner voice is often called the subconscious mind, and it is a source of strength for all people, if you feed it well. Change your words and you'll change your life.

Try using growth mindset phrases like: I'm working on that, I'll figure this out soon, I wonder what I'm missing? And soon you may notice a difference about your thought bubbles. Treat yourself the way you want others to treat you.

The best things in life aren't things. They're living and breathing.

Michael Franti

How often do you pay attention to your breathing?

Taking deep breaths has
proven health benefits:

1) Your muscles relax and let go
of tension. Go ahead, try it.
<pause>
2) Oxygen is delivered quickly to your
cells. Ya know, the life force of all energy.
Cells. With this new oxygen you will notice
better focus and physical endurance.
3) Your blood pressure lowers. When your
muscles release tension the blood vessels
get larger and everything flows more easily.
4) Endorphins are released. You
get some easy happy feelings.
5) It detoxes the junk. There is a whole
system of your body for getting rid of
harmful toxins. Deep breathing helps flush
out germs and builds the army to stand
guard at the door of your mind. Deep
breaths are like little gifts to your body.
Breathe in wisdom. Breathe out worry.

Exercise is more than just physical, it's therapeutic.

Michelle Obama

When you put your body in peak state, how does your mind behave afterwards?

Students who exercise before studying consistently outperform their counterparts. Let's say a room full of people are about to learn 10 new vocabulary words. Half of the people get to play beforehand, while the other half sits and talks to their neighbors.

One group is sweaty, and one group is not. They write and learn their 10 new vocabulary words and, boom! The movement group sends the information into an active part of the brain. The resting group has to settle for reduced power.

The signal speed is kind of like the difference between fast and slow wifi, or worse, dial-up. Quick question: When is the last time you heard someone complain that their internet is too fast? Yeah, me neither. When it comes to learning, faster connection means faster recollection.

The most valuable
lesson we can teach
children is that life is
about the unfolding of
the conscious self.

Shefali Tsabary

How do you show respect
for yourself and listen
to your inner voice?

Silence is full of answers. Today's
wisdom comes from within.

For 15 seconds, try to breathe deeply
and visualize how you would like to treat
yourself, and in turn, for others to treat
you. Our moment of silence starts now...

<note to reader: after 15 silent
seconds...softly talk again>

Breathe deeply.
And so it begins.
And so it is.

Practice makes permanent. Leave perfection to nature.

Jo Giordano

Since very few things can actually be perfect, what if you just went for constant improvement?

<u>Here are some unfortunate mindsets</u>
<u>that slow down growth and learning:</u>
-Stalling before you get started
because it's too overwhelming.
-Blocking creativity by bashing your work.
-Comparing yourself to others.
-Waiting until something is
urgent and rushing through.

Instead, make the move towards
progress and keep it simple and basic
at first. The technique of time-chunking
is really valuable and used often by
leaders. Set a timer for your favorite
number, ideally under 20 minutes so
your attention span can stay focused.

Put the timer near you while you just
get started on something. Once you get
that time-chunk finished, you can set the
timer again for a fun reward, especially
in the form of playful movement. Just
remember, start small but keep going.

Where focus goes energy flows.

Tony Robbins

When you are faced with a tough situation, where does your focus go?

Life gives us interesting challenges for a reason. We would be bored if everyone's life was the same and there were few opportunities to prove our strength.

Obstacles are everywhere in life. They are part of the ride. The way we approach them depends on the kind of person we want to be. Some people take difficulties and resolve them faster than others, with more confidence, happiness, and humor.

<u>When you have something hard in your life going on, ask yourself:</u>
1) What am I going to focus on?
2) What am I going to do?
When you snap your mind
from fear to freedom, you can
change your accomplishments
from "meh" to measurable.

Let food be your medicine.

Vani Hari

How many health benefits can you think of for simply eating apples?

5 benefits of the apple:

1) They contain trace mineral boron. Boron is good for strengthening bones.
2) Apples are a high source of vitamin C which helps build ligaments, tendons, and cartilage. Fewer injuries, more playing.
3) Stomach health. Apples settle stomach sickness.
4) Apples build collagen, which helps skin repair and bounce back from cuts.
5) The fiber in an apple helps you feel full longer and have vibrant energy.

These are just a few of the health benefits of an apple.
Food is energy, and energy is everything.
Be the energy you want to attract.

Physics Law #1
Bodies in motion stay in motion.

Isaac Newton

How often do you let your body surprise and impress you?

Before supermarkets, we had to go out and get our own food by hunting and gathering. This was a time that we were developing into social beings, and our brains were learning to work smarter, not harder.

We used to run or walk 12 or more miles a day in order to find success. We won the survival of the fittest contest. Here are a few of the skills we can thank exercise for bringing to our species: planning and predicting, organizing our materials, stopping in the moment and shifting to another activity, controlling our emotions, and self-regulating.

Next time you're feeling a little off, ask yourself if you have given your brain the movement it needs. Human beings are not meant to sit for very long. Nothing in the universe rests; everything moves. More steps, more flex, more self-respect.

Be as radiant as the sun,
as generous as a tree.

Michael Franti

Would it bring you peace
to discover we have the
same DNA as trees?

Ancient civilizations have always known that a tree has wisdom. In Japan, they launched a national health program prescribing folks to spend more time around trees. No jogging, no climbing, just quietly being near trees.

Studies show that this practice dubbed "forest bathing" lowered depression, stress hormones, and heart and blood pressure. They also found that being around trees strengthens our immune system and boosts energy.

Most forests we walk through are older than we realize. They are filled with ancient giants who provide us with the basic human need of oxygen. When you take a deep breath of relaxation, thank the trees. Connect to source, sync your system.

You've got seconds to grab your audience's attention and only minutes to keep it.

John Medina

How can we use laughter in our classrooms to keep us focused and healthy?

Life is better when you are laughing. Your doctor wants you to prioritize it. Also, it looks real good on you. Walking around all serious and worried is like walking around with an umbrella all the time waiting for it to rain - not your best look.

Put your thoughts on the good things in life. You have a shorter distance to travel to laughing. Smile. You are sending a physiological message to your brain and it will change your state of mind.

Spend time with fun, playful people. Every comedian appreciates an audience. Bring humor into conversations. Ask people, "What's the funniest thing that happened to you this week?" Laughter is an instant vacation and is said to be the shortest distance between two people. Keep it light, put down the fight, the pursuit of happiness is your given right.

Conscious thoughts, repeated often enough, become unconscious thinking.

Joe Dispenza

What are your top 3 habits that serve you well?

When you want to be in great shape, you don't just work out for a week and then consider it done. The same goes for emotional health. Habits are essential. When successful people are interviewed, here are the common health habits that serve them well:

1) Bring a water bottle everywhere.
2) Find a way to be quiet and still with yourself for a little while every day. Many people use a morning meditation and visualization practice.
3) Write in a gratitude journal for 10 minutes a day.
4) Leave screens out of the bedroom and shut them off 2 hours before bedtime. Science shows it makes for better sleep.
5) Compliment 3 people on who they are on the inside: their character traits.
6) Move your body, both for physical health and mental well-being. First we make our habits, then our habits make us.

Optimism is a muscle, it gets stronger with use.

Robin Roberts

Do your friends talk about positive ideas?

The doctor would want you to pick good people for your health. Social connection is one of the top ways to create a positive feedback loop of self-esteem and empathy. Happy friendships lead to healthy people.

Sadly, the opposite is true with drama-filled and unhealthy friendships. They can be terrible for your mind and body. There is a phrase that says, "some people major in minor things." That means people focus on negative and weak subjects, in a big way.

Experts say to listen carefully to what your friends bring up in conversation. If they are talking bad about another person, there is a good chance that they would talk poorly about you as well. Hang with a crowd that likes to talk about ideas and not talk bad about people. Be sure: who you hang beside will bring you pride.

You know the truth
by the way it feels.

India Arie

Do you know how your
body feels when you
need more water?

Our bodies are more than half water. We rely on the strength of water for living. The human body can go for weeks without food but only a few days without water.

<u>Here are some of the benefits
to being hydrated:</u>
1) Your head is clear and free of headaches.
2) Better immune system
and less getting sick.
3) All functions of learning improve when you drink water. If you lose even 1-3% of your fluids, you have less brain function.
4) Better motivation and more energy.
5) Better mood.

Listen for the phrases that might tell you to drink more water. Usually they sound like: "I don't care, I don't feel like it, I'm too tired, I have no idea, I'm in a bad mood." Chances are, you're dehydrated. Charge your battery. Plug into the power source.

What we dwell on is who we become.

Oprah Winfrey

When people around you get angry, do you fall into the trap to join them?

Getting upset, frustrated, or angry might seem to pass pretty quickly, but your body takes about 2 hours to recover from the stress. For some people, it takes even longer. When we lose our temper, our heart rate gets higher. Cortisol pumps through our body and disrupts our circuit board for a little while.

Cortisol is a stress hormone that scrambles learning, memory, and well-being. Worse, your body is working too hard to figure out how to settle the storm and cannot focus on health. Most immune systems are weak for people who get angry or frustrated easily. Stress makes us sick.

Find a way to avoid stressful situations and people. Your health depends on it. So, let's ditch the sick clinic and have an attitude of gratitude.

Your life unfolds in proportion to your courage.

Danielle LaPorte

If you could ask for one wish, what would it be?

A poem for inspiration:

Courage is the strength to stand up
When it's easier to fall down and lose hold.
It is the conviction to explore new horizons
when it's easier to believe what we've been told.
Courage is the desire to maintain our integrity
when it's easier to look the other way.
It is feeling happy and alive, and moving forward
when it's easier to feel sorry for ourselves and stay.
Courage is the will to shape our world
When it's easier to let someone else do it for us.
It is the recognition that none of us are perfect
When it's easier to criticize others and fuss.
Courage is the power to step forward and lead
when it's easier to follow the crowd;
their pleas resound.
It is the spirit that places you on top of the mountain
when it's easier to never leave the ground.
The foundation of courage is solid,
the rock that doesn't roll.
Courage is the freedom
of our mind, body, and soul.

-Anonymous

We do not inherit
the Earth from our
parents. We borrow it
from our children.

Native American Proverb

Do you strive for a
greater good?

The language we use is powerful. Listen closely to hear what follows the word "should". "I should go over and help that person" is not enough. Often it ISN'T the thought that counts, but rather the action.

The same goes when we tell ourselves we should do something, but we're too tired. A real common phrase from many people is, "I know I should exercise, but I'm too tired." Or, "I know I should do more for the environment, but it's too overwhelming."

If you look closer at the science of exercise, you would discover that you actually gain more energy, if you do it right. If you think about the food we put into our body, you either get strength or sickness from the ingredients. Less talking and more doing paves the path to successful living.

Let food be your medicine.

Vani Hari

How many health benefits can you think of for simply eating carrots?

<u>5 health benefits of the carrot:</u>
1) They can relax tension in your
blood vessels and arteries.
2) Carrots boost circulation
which helps organs.
3) They are a rich source of vitamin C,
which keeps us from getting sick.
4) Carrots are a rich source of vitamin
A through beta-carotene, which
is helpful for strong eyesight.
5) They have good minerals for oral
health and avoiding cavities.

These are just a few of the
health benefits of a carrot.
Food is energy, and energy is everything.
Be the energy you want to attract.

"The knowing" is that sense that lives within all of us; we know when we are going in the right direction and we know when something is off.

Joy Harjo

----- -----

----- -----

----- -----

What would you do with your life if you knew there were no limits?

Decisions based on fear are usually the wrong ones. There are a few key questions to ask yourself when trying to make a big choice:

1) A year from now, will this matter?
2) Which path will make me feel most proud?
3) How does my body feel when I think about the options? Which one makes me feel uncomfortable, tight, and uneasy? Which one makes me sit up tall and drop my shoulders down?

Big choices come with a lot of emotion. It's okay to be scared. Being scared means you're about to do something really, really brave. Be brave now because things will get better. It may be stormy now, but it can't rain forever. On the other side of fear is your destiny. Jump the fence.

If you change the way you look at things, the things you look at change.

Wayne Dyer

- - - - -

- - - - -

- - - - -

Is there something stressful you can move past today, just by facing it differently?

Have you ever noticed that we make school assignments harder than they need to be by putting them off until the last minute? Our idea of how hard they are becomes bigger and bigger. The same goes for studying for a test. Here are scientific reasons that cramming doesn't work:

1) Rushing and hurrying to fit in information is done with stress. This blocks our strong memory skills.
2) Our brain, at night, puts information in the right places so we can find them when the time is right. We need a few good nights of sleep with repeated studying to really store information.
3) If it isn't interesting, your brain will likely dump it. This is why you cannot remember what you ate for breakfast two weeks ago.

Cramming is usually boring and stressful. That's just not going to convince your brain to remember. Take time to make your learning fun, and you'll remember it. Don't stress, do your best, ace the test.

One child, one teacher, one book, one pen can change the world.

Malala Yousafzai

If you could teach groups of people, what would you talk about?

Silence is full of answers. Today's wisdom comes from within.

For 15 seconds, try to breathe deeply and visualize yourself being a master of something and teaching others. Our moment of silence starts now...

<note to reader: after 15 silent seconds...softly talk again>

Breathe deeply.
And so it begins.
And so it is.

Seek the feedback in the areas of life that you're open to improvement.

Mel Robbins

How do you listen and accept peoples' opinions and advice?

We cannot control others, only ourselves. Sometimes we get really great advice from people, and sometimes we get lousy feedback. Accept them both with grace. Don't take things so personally. Someone's opinion of you is a reflection usually based on how they feel about themselves, not about you.

<u>Here are some tips to know if another person is giving you good solid advice with a bit of "tough-love" spice:</u>
1) They may say things that are hard to hear, but they say it with kindness.
2) They look you in the eyes and speak to you with respect.
3) You can tell that they put themselves in your shoes and are trying to help based on their experience. Push skip on a low-quality tip. Push play on an upgrade pathway.

There is no reason to constantly attempt to figure everything out.

Michael Singer

What if we could solve disagreements with games?

The Olympics brings people together from all different countries, even the ones that don't get along very well. Play is the universal language. We can put disagreements aside for a little while, in order to get to common ground. Next time you have a conflict, and two people both want to talk, try an active version of rock paper scissors before talking about the issue. The ice-breaker serves a purpose. When in doubt, play it out.

The science behind this is remarkable. Endorphins like serotonin help your mood while GABA helps calm you down. It sure is better than coming into a conversation fired up, frustrated, and brain-bamboozled with fog. Play is powerful for peacemaking.

For the smaller issues, less exercise is needed. Perhaps that's where we got the phrase, "don't sweat the small stuff." Movement manages the mayhem in our mind.

If we take away the labels, we realize that we are far more alike than we are different.

Ellen DeGeneres

----- ----- -----

Who in your life surprised you once you got to know them?

There are good labels and lousy ones. The tags that help us organize are fabulous. Putting a label on a person just doesn't make sense though. It's like the phrase, "Don't judge a book by its cover." It's messy to make assumptions about folks.

Accepting people as people, that's a clean scene for the heart. What else in your life would be so much easier if it was simple and less messy?

6 ways to declutter your mind:
1. Clean up your physical space.
2. Forgive yourself.
3. Go outside.
4. Get rid of what you don't use.
5. Stop overbooking yourself.
6. Write everything that's going on in your head on a piece of paper.
The simplest things can bring the most happiness.
Bring it back to basics.

Life is found in the dance between your deepest desire and your greatest fear.

Tony Robbins

Can you keep your cool while being uncomfortable?

Fear is a part of life. Everyone battles with their own stuff. However, if most of your decisions are made out of fear, you are missing out on your greatest self. The trick is to understand what scares you and train your mind to move past it.

What if you gave up on yourself when you were learning to walk or talk? "Oooh, oooh, you're almost there - oh, bummer you're no good at that. Maybe it's not your thing." No. Instead, we celebrate the small successes towards our goals and keep training ourselves to move past fear.

What if we viewed failure as one of our greatest teachers? Play with it and consider it as a lesson that we are on the track to something great. The strongest people are not necessarily those who show strength in front of the world, but who fight and win battles that others know nothing about.

Integrity is doing the right thing, knowing that nobody will know whether you did it or not.

Oprah Winfrey

How often do you give without expecting anything in return?

We earn the trust of friendship when we are living with integrity. Folks are looking to hang out with people who make their life stronger. Giving and being generous without expecting anything in return goes a long way for building trust. Serve the world with your joy.

A few fun facts about friendships:
- Good friendships can mean you live longer.
- It is scientifically proven that spending time with your friends reduces stress and anxiety.
- Even young babies learn these relationship emotions before learning to walk or talk.
- Friend lifestyles, especially around exercise and nutrition, are contagious. When one friend decides to get fit and healthy, the others rise up as well.

Give and take is fair play. Make sure good friendships are part of your health plan each day.

All physical changes that we are in search of have a mental, emotional, and spiritual origin.

Angela M. Davis

Why do so many leaders in the world recommend yoga and meditation?

Many say that connecting the left and right sides of the brain, with intentional practices, can help the mind be more in the present moment. The right side is stronger with intuition and imagination; the left side is stronger with facts and sequencing. As a learner, we want the creative side to talk to the logical side. Neurons that fire together, wire together.

Try this: take the left hand and reach over to touch the right hip, and bring it back. Now do the same thing with the right hand. Do about 20 of those cycles to awaken the connections between the left and right hemisphere.

You can switch the movements and adapt to cross with different body parts. By crossing the mid-line you'll find more self-control, concentration, and expanded learning. Be your own boss. Own the business of your brain.

We don't have to understand electricity to appreciate the lights being on.

Bob Proctor

What are some basic things you remember to notice?

10 things we often take for granted most days:

1) You woke up breathing. Huge bonus.

2) Food and water are only a few minutes away, and people around you notice if you need it.

3) We are young and can make choices for our future success.

4) Our senses: you may not have all of them but give thanks for the ones you do. Hearing, seeing, smelling, tasting, and feeling are often overlooked.

5) Our body is designed to heal itself.

6) Books. We didn't even have to write them to enjoy them.

7) People surround us. We are creatures of connection, and it's a gift to have human interaction. Did you know that one of the greatest forms of sadness and pain is to constantly be alone? No thanks.

8) Music. A good song can uplift our mood.

9) Nature. We may or may not have a whole lot of it around us, but we have enough to give us oxygen. Plus there is beauty in nature that is nothing short of miraculous.

10) An education. We are on the path that many do not get to take. Being well-educated will absolutely improve our future.

Let food be your medicine.

Vani Hari

How many health benefits can you think of for simply eating bananas?

5 benefits of the banana:

1) They contain vitamin B9 which is called folate. It helps the feel-good natural chemical serotonin enter the brain faster. This means they help us to be more happy and fight depression.
2) Bananas are a high source of potassium. Fewer sore muscles, more playing.
3) They are good for your eye health.
4) Bananas are a quick source of natural sugar. There is a reason folks eat bananas before a race. They are rich in glucose.
5) They are a high source of iron, which gives your cells oxygen so you can have more energy.

Those are just a few of the health benefits of a banana. Food is energy, and energy is everything. Be the energy you want to attract.

We must keep the promises that we make to ourselves, so that we can keep those that we make to other people.

Jay Shetty

Are you following the crowd or making your own decisions?

Let's imagine you could interview all the living grandmothers of students in this school. The wisdom would be legit! If you asked them which decisions shaped their lives, you would learn a lot. Many probably would tell you that they wished they made one big move sooner than they did. Why do we wait so long to follow our bliss?

There is something unique inside of you. We don't often recognize it, because we are so busy trying to fit in and be like everyone else. Find your hidden talent. What do you love to do?

Everyone has a purpose. Your calling is your gift, and it is often hidden by muting our inner voice. Listen. Seek passion. Make bold decisions towards your deep desires. Decide what you want and get busy. Fortune favors the brave.

80% of life is for creating
your ideal situation.
20% is for cleansing
and purifying.

Danielle LaPorte

How do you let others
lead so you can
replenish your energy?

<u>Here are some life lessons from geese when they are flying in a V-formation:</u>

-As each goose flaps its wings, it creates an uplift for the birds that follow. By flying in a V-formation, the whole flock achieves a 70% greater flying range than if they flew alone.

-When the lead goose gets tired, it rotates to the back of the formation and allows the others to take the lead.

-When a goose gets sick or wounded, two other geese drop out of formation and follow it down to help and protect it. They stay with it until it passes away or is able to fly again.

-They stay committed to their values. Their migration routes never change. They use the same path year after year. Even when the flock members change, the young learn the route from their parents. In the spring they will go back to the spot where they were born.

Learn from the geese. Remember you need self-care to recharge and repair.

It is a privilege and honor for leaders to take care of people. All lives, no matter where they live on the planet, are equal and we need to treat them as such.

Melinda Gates

Are you grateful for the right to an education?

Silence is full of answers. Today's wisdom comes from within.

For 15 seconds, try to breathe deeply and give thanks for something in your school year that is going well. Our moment of silence starts now...

<note to reader: after 15 silent seconds...softly talk again>

Breathe deeply.
And so it begins.
And so it is.

It's remarkable how much power one good person can have in shaping the life of a child. Having great teachers is key.

Bill Gates

What is one thing you wish your teacher knew about you?

Try to really get to know 3 teachers before you leave this school year. You will likely be impressed by the exchange of conversation. Some reminders about the kind of person who chooses to teach: They sacrifice their needs for the needs of their students. They give love, attention, and time to kids who aren't even their own. They're adaptable and resourceful. They choose every day to work on building the future leaders of tomorrow. They ask great questions. Some of the most important questions they ask are about us as people. They may be hard on us, but that's because they want us to be strong leaders to go out and make positive change. Those folks who are tough enough to believe they can change the world will likely be the exact ones who do. Remember that teachers are living that very same dream by dedicating their hard days to us. Breathe deeply with gratitude.

Successful people ask better questions, and as a result, they get better answers.

Tony Robbins

Do your questions add value to those around you?

An old book gives advice for winning friends and working well with people. Here are the main suggestions:
1) Become interested in other people. Ask questions that get folks talking about their personal lives and hobbies.
2) Smile. When your smile muscles contract, they send a signal to the back of your brain that releases endorphins simply from smiling, as it tells your brain you are happy. Being happy is a magnet for others.
3) Remember a person's name and use it in conversation.
4) Be a good listener. Encourage people to talk about themselves.
5) Ask good questions to bring out the best in other people. If you can get them to stand tall, you are winning.

Just as you do for others, ask yourself hard questions, never stop asking, and let your answers change as you do.

If you see someone without a smile, give them one of yours.

Dolly Parton

How do you spread joy?

We hear people continually point out that negative thoughts are super unhealthy and they begin to manifest into our reality. It is sometimes hard to control. People nearby affect us, the songs affect us, the videos affect us.

How do we keep changing our thoughts when things around us keep happening that really bring us down? If you want freedom from this happening to you, remember that change happens from the inside out...not the outside in.

You will never ever be able to control others. You can only control your reaction to others. Consider that any time you think that the problem is "out there" or with circumstances, that very thought is the problem. It is better to light a candle than to be upset with the darkness. Happiness is an inside job, with premium benefits.

Life gives you an endless supply of do-overs.

Iyanla Vanzant

How do you talk to yourself when you make a mistake?

<u>Here are some phrases that block growth:</u>
This is the way I've always been.
Why do I always do that?
How does this always happen to me?
Why am I always trying to catch up?
Things just never work the way I want.
I am never going to get this.
You never listen to me.

These types of phrases use language that puts a block on growth, and often they are just not true. We are changing every day, so who is to say what will never or always be in our life? Let's be more honest with ourselves. We are moving towards what we want. Forward is still forward.

A year from today you'll be glad you started now. Try changing your language to flip negative words into the positive version like rephrase "never give up" to "keep going when it's hard." Words are free. It's how you use them that may cost you.

Do what you **have** to until you can do what you **want** to.

Oprah Winfrey

What is your hardest class this year?

If it doesn't challenge you, it doesn't change you. When you raise your standards, you'll notice that your dreams become slightly harder to reach, because they're bigger dreams. Reach for them anyway.

When you are confused by subjects, you have to study longer to learn them. Learn them anyway.
When you have a friend who takes longer to earn their trust, you have to be patient and work harder proving that you are trustworthy. Work harder anyway.

Most things are difficult before you get used to it. Nobody said a good life would be easy. They said it would be worth it. Push on past your edge, past the tough parts. What you want, deep down, will be on the other side of hard work. Dig in deep and get going.

If you don't have anything helpful to say about something, you don't have to speak.

Gayle King

Can you pick one bad habit and let it go?

Make a decision about something that doesn't serve you. Examples: being late, rushing at the last minute to get things done, talking about a person when they aren't around to defend themselves. Take a moment to pick something.
<pause>

Just like that you can be done with it. Forgive yourself for the way it interrupted your flow, and move on. Change is never a matter of ability; it is a matter of decision and motivation.

Create a new empowering pattern and reinforce it until it is a habit. Keep yourself motivated with notes and remember this is your choice. We all get what we tolerate in ourselves. Decide, commit. Tell that habit you're done with it.

If you talk about it, it's a dream. If you envision it, it's possible. If you schedule it, it's real.

Tony Robbins

When was the last time you made a bold move for your future dream?

Keep talking about the goals you want in your life. Using growth language continues to drive the momentum forward. Some key phrases are: I'm working on, I'm in the process of, I'm getting closer to, and I am moving towards.

As you continually vocalize your desires, also be sure to schedule something that is slightly out of your comfort zone. Each time you make another bold move, you are getting closer to making the end goal into a reality.

The most crucial days are the ones where you decide to play extra big in life: sign up for a team, ask the person the question, schedule the future race and start training for it, fill out the paperwork for a scholarship. Set your sights on what you want and build your life around that. Put success on your schedule.

Let food be your medicine.

Vani Hari

How many health benefits can you think of for simply eating broccoli?

5 benefits of broccoli:

1) It is rich in vitamin K and choline (Ko-Leen) which boost brain health and memory.

2) It's an alkaline vegetable that balances our body's PH.

3) Broccoli is good for your eye health.

4) It is rich in calcium, magnesium, and potassium for bone and teeth health.

5) Broccoli is rich in vitamin A and Omega-3 fatty acids that are helpful for glowing and healthy skin.

These are just a few of the health benefits of broccoli.
Food is energy, and energy is everything.
Be the energy you want to attract.

People are rewarded in public for what they practice in private.

Tony Robbins

What is your hobby that you practice while no one is around?

Very rarely do we celebrate a person who did something well for the first time. Often a person becomes great after practice, lots of practice. It can be difficult to stick with something for a little bit every day. Many people get frustrated when they don't see results quickly enough. That is one major difference between feeling low and feeling like a pro.

So, what would you practice
more if you thought it could lead
to your future happiness?
-playing an instrument?
-telling jokes?
-soccer juggling?
Leaders drop clues that we can follow.
Start reading about your favorite people
who are doing what you want to do.
Guaranteed that they will claim practice
got them where they are. Repetition is the
birthplace of a skill. Make time for practice.

Sometimes the bravest
and most important
thing you can do
is just show up.

Brené Brown

- - - - -

- - - - -

- - - - -

Where could you show
up more in your life?

Silence is full of answers. Today's wisdom comes from within.

For 15 seconds, try to breathe deeply and imagine doing something outrageous that would make you immensely proud. Our moment of silence starts now...

<note to reader: after 15 silent seconds...softly talk again>

Breathe deeply.
And so it begins.
And so it is.

What the mind can conceive and believe, it can achieve.

Napoleon Hill

Can the brain tell the difference between real and imaginary?

When award-winning athletes are hooked up so their brain activity can be analyzed, we learn so much about the power of the brain. The athletes are asked to close their eyes and visualize the sport event that would be ideal to them. The results are absolutely amazing.

The act of crafting it in the mind, with vivid details, is just the same as actually performing it. Even their heart rate and breathing changes to adapt to the movie they are creating in their mind. These findings quickly convinced athletes to add mental training to their workout.

Stretching and pre-game meditation is possibly the most important part of their routine, and likely their best-kept secret. Picture the thing you want, see it, feel it, believe in it. Make your mental blueprint, and begin to build.

You become who you
spend time with.

Tony Robbins

- - - - -

- - - - -

- - - - -

Who do you look
up to and why?

<u>Here are 7 tips for choosing people that are best to be spending time with:</u>
- Folks with similar goals.
- Folks who can bring balance where you are not as strong.
- People who motivate and challenge you.
- People who are hungry for knowledge.
- Folks who are happy for you when you do something well.

- You also want people who are sad for you when life is hard, but do not let you stay upset too long. They focus on the positive.
- They are movers and shakers. People who build friendships with movement have deep connections because dopamine is released. Sports teammates are bonded for many science-based reasons.

To have good friends, be one first. Give people the chance to surprise and impress you, even if you weren't sure about them before. Friends are the family you choose.

Healthy people create peaceful countries.

Alaa Murabit

Do you realize how many countries struggle to have clean drinking water?

Amazing facts about water:
- Our brains are 75% water.
- 70% of the Earth's surface is water.
- Our bodies are 60-70% water.
- By the time you're thirsty you're already dehydrated.
- Only 1 in 4 adults in the US are properly hydrated.
- Only 1 in 7 people in the world have access to clean drinking water.

So, let's take advantage of this great privilege and life source. A fun game to get the gulps in is called waterfall.

Try this later when the time is right. In a group of 4 or 5 people, a circle is formed with water bottles filled. The leader is established. Everyone says "cheers" and starts to drink. After a few seconds the leader puts theirs down, then the person to their left, then the person to their left, and so on until the last person gets to put down their water bottle. Get your fill, respect the swill.

I never lose.
I either win or learn.

Nelson Mandela

What lessons in life did you learn the hard way?

Evidently, lessons we learn get easier with time. Just like muscles need training, so does our adaptability and resilience.

<u>Top 10 internal habits that are trained when you are a student athlete:</u>
- perseverance - responsibility
- commitment - patience
- time management - empathy
- moving on from the past - integrity
- endurance - goal setting

Whether you choose a team sport or individual activity, keep reaching for a sport that uses numbers and has the ability for you to beat your personal best. Do not let anyone tell you that you are not athletic, because you haven't been alive long enough to allow someone to define who you are or are not. After years of training, decide what's true. You be you.

When we take care of ourselves, we can be even better at taking care of others and fulfilling our work.

Latham Thomas

Do you prioritize healthy sleep for yourself?

Did you know that there are people who write down their dreams and study them? Some inventions, theories, songs, and books came from people's dream studies.

Here's a short list of amazing discoveries that were born from dreamland:
- The idea for Google
- The typewriter
- The song "Yesterday" by the Beatles
- The characters of Twilight
- The periodic table
- The image and shape of DNA
- The theory of relativity
- The character Frankenstein
- The structure of the atom
- Benzene molecule

Some tips for getting a good dream cycle would be to go to sleep the same time every night, stay away from screen devices for 2 hours before bed, make your sleep area as comfortable and quiet as you can, and say your gratitude as you close your eyes. Rest, relax, enjoy the deep of sleep.

The secret to living is giving.

Tony Robbins

What job would you like to have when you're an adult?

As an adult, the working world can be really rewarding. Earning money can be fun. That said, we often hear that people were not taught about making and managing money, and they wish someone had explained some basics in school.

<u>Here are some fundamentals:</u>
- The more you learn, the more you earn. Stay in school and take hard classes. It may literally pay off later.
- Most people who earn a lot of money say that they are most proud to give gifts to other people. Yes, you heard that right. A research project on happiness provided a free 5 dollar bill to people and asked them to spend it on themselves or another person. The ones who spent money on others were measurably happier. Your brain's pleasure and reward center lights up as if you were the one who received it. The secret to living is giving.

You get in life whatever you have the courage to ask for.

Oprah Winfrey

Do you believe you are worthy of asking for great things?

Silence is full of answers. Today's wisdom comes from within.

For 15 seconds, try to breathe deeply and visualize how you want one goal to look and feel in your life. Our moment of silence starts now...

<note to reader: after 15 silent seconds...softly talk again>

Breathe deeply.
And so it begins.
And so it is.

Let food be your medicine.

Vani Hari

How many health benefits can you think of for simply eating strawberries?

<u>5 benefits of the strawberry:</u>
1) They are high in omega-3s which boosts short-term memory. That could help with something you are trying to memorize quickly.
2) The acid whitens your teeth, removes tartar, and strengthens gums.
3) Strawberries are great for your heart health.
4) They are a good source of vitamin K which is good for your bones. Fewer injuries, more playing.
5) Strawberries are rich in iodine which is helpful for your thyroid. This gland plays a big role in the metabolism and energy of your body.

These are just a few of the health benefits of a strawberry.
Food is energy, and energy is everything.
Be the energy you want to attract.

Be stingy with your
time and spend it in
spaces that fill you up.

Janet Mock

If your life was a
movie, would you
enjoy watching it?

When someone asks you how you are doing, what do you say? What would it take to make it an amazing response? If you don't love your answer, do you have the courage to start over and change the movie of your life?

When you raise your standards, you'll notice that you tolerate less junk and your dreams become slightly harder to reach, because they're bigger dreams. Reach for them anyway. When people ask you how you're doing, you have to think harder and train your language to focus on gratitude. Think harder anyway.

Most things are difficult at first. Nobody said a good life would be easy, they said it would be worth it. Only tolerate discomfort as you strive for excellence. Push through past your edge. On the other side of fear is your destiny. Jump the fence. Live with passion.

Gratitude is the single most important ingredient to living a successful and fulfilled life.

Jack Canfield

What are you grateful for?

Saying "thank you" may be the reason for your success. Scientists have proven that saying your gratitude has results: it makes you more happy, more physically fit, sleep better, recover from trauma, lowers anger, and you have more empathy.

Try a thank you card to yourself. Write down 10 basic parts of your life that make it easier to live with comfort. If you are struggling to come up with 10 try scanning your body from the bottom to the top.

Do you have the ability to be grateful for something you never had to lose? You don't have to learn all the lessons yourself; you can look around at others and realize how good you have it. Be the one who knows the difference between "compare" and "aware" and between "wishful" and "thankful".

Dream big and your problems become small.

Vishen Lakhiani

What is your biggest dream in your life?

Get serious about your desires. Imagine you get to write a story with you as the main character. Try playing through the script like an artist. Sculpt, draft, sketch, step back, see how it looks and feels.

What if your biggest dream is just waiting for you to put it in action? What if you did have power to design it through your constant and active goal setting?

Even if you simply learn more clues that get you closer, forward is still forward. A goal-setting session with friends and family is a work of art. It's a great big canvas waiting for you to throw lots of paint. Don't worry about how you should draw it, just draw it the way you see it. It's your goal, your soul, and in your control.

Every time you find
humor in a difficult
situation, you win.

Would you consider
yourself a funny person?

Laughter and play bond us together. It is a hidden language that we all speak, and it is genetic. Anyone who has ever laughed at the sight of another person giggling really hard can agree: laughter is contagious. Of course it is hardest to keep a situation light when we are in a difficult hang-up. Some people still find a way. That is the mark of true genius.

It is also what relationship experts say is a great way to build back and repair good feelings between people. Find a way to joke and play, and your hard times may quickly fade away.

Pro tip: The easiest way to disarm a bully is to take any insult they say to you and follow it with, "I know and isn't it hilarious". Keep laughing at yourself. When you mess up, when you fall, the reaction is your call. Find joy in your new point of view.

A well-spent day brings happy sleep.

Leonardo da Vinci

Do you consider yourself well-rested?

Interesting facts about sleep:

- Lack of sleep over time can actually shrink your brain.
- Parents of newborn babies miss out on 6 months of sleep in their child's first 2 years of life.
- Cell phone radiation causes insomnia. Using your phone before bed can prevent you from getting sleep. Best to put it outside of your room and give your brain a break.
- If you don't get enough sleep per night you are more likely to lie, cheat, and steal.
- Albert Einstein demanded 10 hours of sleep per night.
- A good night's sleep improves your mood, energy, concentration, immune system, weight management, physical health, decision making skills, ability to manage stress, and memory.

Relax your pulse: hit the horizontals.

Trust that everything happens for a reason, even if we are not wise enough to see it.

Oprah Winfrey

\- - - - -

\- - - - -

\- - - - -

What did you learn yesterday?

10 life lessons from inspired by the Dalai Lama:

1. The purpose of life is to be happy.
2. Happiness is not ready made. It comes from our actions.
3. Be kind whenever possible. It is always possible.
4. Well-being comes through action.
5. Sleep is the best meditation.
6. Love and compassion are necessities, not luxuries. Without them humanity cannot survive.
7. In the practice of tolerance, one's enemy is the best teacher.
8. When you practice gratefulness, there is a sense of respect towards others.
9. Where ignorance is our master, there is no possibility of real peace.
10. A more compassionate mind, more sense of concern for other's well-being, is a source of happiness.

Success is its own
reward, but failure is
a great teacher too,
and not to be feared.

Sonia Sotomayor

Which is worse: failing or
never giving it a shot?

Silence is full of answers. Today's wisdom comes from within.

For 15 seconds, try to breathe deeply and visualize how you want one goal to look and feel in your life. Our moment of silence starts now...

<note to reader: after 15 silent seconds...softly talk again>

Breathe deeply.
And so it begins.
And so it is.

Yesterday I was clever so I wanted to change the world. Today I am wise so I want to change myself.

Rumi

How can you be the change you wish to see in the world?

Gandhi

Often we need to remember our wise from within. Our brain is the strongest computer ever invented. As a student, you are declaring your intelligence as your superpower. Some even think that kids have a special wisdom that adults wish they still had.

Adults often say, "I wish I had half of their energy." Students learn so much in a year. It's truly amazing how much you expand your knowledge in a decade of life. How do you keep growing so rapidly? Many researchers conclude that exercise is why kids can learn so much. There is something called BDNF that magnifies learning opportunities in your brain.

How does exercise enhance learning? Let's remember together: It builds new brain cells, improves memory, lengthens attention span, improves planning and decision-making skills, and wakes you up from a cellular level. If it entertains you, it sustains you.

Forgive yourself for your faults and mistakes and move on.

Les Brown

What is one issue you want to move past?

Your past mistakes are meant to guide you, not define you. The time to forgive is now.

In one African tribe, when someone does something harmful, they take the person to the center of the village where the whole tribe comes and surrounds them. For two days, they will say to the person all the good things that he or she has done. The tribe believes that each human being comes into the world as good. Each one of us only desires safety, love, peace, and happiness. But sometimes, in the pursuit of these things, people make mistakes. The community sees those mistakes as a cry for help. They unite to lift the person up, to reconnect them with their true nature, to remind them who they really are.
The truth is: I am good.

As you go on today, remember to forgive and forget. Scientifically, forgiveness is a direct line to happiness.

Let food be your medicine.

Vani Hari

\- - - - - -

\- - - - -

\- - - - - -

How many health benefits can you think of for simply eating tomatoes?

<u>Here are 5 benefits of the tomato:</u>
1) They are high in vitamin C for staying healthy. A single tomato can provide about 40% of the daily vitamin C requirement.
2) Vitamin A in tomatoes is excellent for your vision.
3) They are great for your heart health and lower cholesterol.
4) Tomatoes are a good source of vitamin K, which is good for healing cuts. Fewer injuries, more playing.
5) They are great for your hair and skin. Even putting tomato juice directly on sunburn can help soothe the skin.

These are just a few of the health benefits of a tomato. Food is energy, and energy is everything. Be the energy you want to attract.

Do the best you can until you know better. When you know better, do better.

Maya Angelou

- - - - -

- - - - -

- - - - -

How do your teachers inspire you to improve?

<u>Here are interesting facts about teachers:</u>
37% of school teachers in the US use their personal money to feed their students. They spend an average of $35 a month. With 3.1 million teachers in the US, that means that American teachers are spending $400 million of their personal money on hungry students.

Another form of teacher currency is how they dedicate time to their students during off-hours. Often they are the most humble people and you would never know the dedication that goes on behind the scenes.

A recent study conducted by the National Education Association asked teachers what they would want most from their students and 50% of the responses said a simple thank you card. It takes a big heart to shape young minds. A true hero is measured not by the size of their strength, but the size of their heart. What unique way can you thank a teacher today?

Imagination is more important than knowledge. Knowledge is limited. Imagination encircles the world.

Albert Einstein

If you could send the world a message, what would you say in 30 seconds?

<u>7 Life lessons inspired by Einstein:</u>
1. Follow your curiosity. He said,
"I have no special talent. I am
only passionately curious."
2. Perseverance is priceless. You do
not necessarily need to be the person
with the highest IQ, but rather the one
who stays with problems the longest.
3. Make mistakes. Great inventors
and leaders see mistakes as a metric
of trying something new. Our fear
factor of failure can be lower, if we
get used to making more mistakes.
4. Create value. Einstein said, "The value
of a man should be seen in what he gives
and not in what he is able to receive."
5. Knowledge comes from experience.
Information is not knowledge. Live to learn,
and pursue your passion. Experience your
wisdom by living a healthy and happy life.
6. Learn the rules and then play better. If
life is a game, play at the highest level.

Albert Einstein name and quotes used with permission
of ©The Hebrew University of Jerusalem

Sometimes not getting what you want is a wonderful stroke of luck.

Dalai Lama

How often do you compare yourself to other people and what they have?

There will be folks who have more than you, and the temptation will be to wonder why it didn't come to you. Some people will have the latest and shiniest devices, and toys that make you green with envy.

You are given the feelings of jealousy to test your inner strength. It's almost like a trick or a temptation to see if you fall for it. The envy of a friend is termed "frenvy" and the struggle is real. It doesn't have to be a bad emotion unless you choose to dwell on it or do something mean. Being at peace with your own self is the number one way to snap out of jealousy. When you stop comparing yourself to others, you allow your light to be bright. The stars do not compare themselves to the sun, they all shine when it's their time.

The quote, "If a train doesn't stop at your station, then it's not your train" could be a reminder that we have major blessings ahead. The ones intended for us will come in their own time. How you act, while you wait, could be the test of the most blessed.

When you have a vision,
stand for it, stand with
it. Even if it means you
have to stand by yourself.

Iyanla Vanzant

If you could be one of the
most influential people
in the world, what would
you change and why?

Silence is full of answers. Today's wisdom comes from within.

For 15 seconds, try to breathe deeply and visualize how you want one vision to look and feel in your life. Our moment of silence starts now...

<note to reader: after 15 silent seconds...softly talk again>

Breathe deeply.
And so it begins.
And so it is.

Education is the key to unlocking the world, a passport to freedom.

Oprah Winfrey

If your school could do a virtual conversation with another classroom in any country, which country would you choose?

A poem for inspiration:
Plant three rows of peas.
Peace of mind
Peace of heart
Peace of soul

Plant three rows of squash
Squash gossip
Squash grumbling
Squash hate

Plant three rows of lettuce
Lettuce be kind
Lettuce be patient
Lettuce really love one another

Plant three rows of turnips
Turnips for meetings
Turnips for service
Turnip to help one another

Water freely with patience and
cultivate with love.
There is much fruit in your garden
because you reap what you sow.
- Anonymous

As you go down the mountain, put the brake on when you need it, rather than dragging the brake all the way down.

Mike Sinyard

Can you appreciate forward momentum and just enjoy the ride?

Find at least one sport that gives you the sensation that time flies by. Even bigger life bonus if you actually feel like you are flying when doing it.

A few outdoor sports where people have claimed it feels like they are floating in the wind are: skiing and snowboarding, surfing, wakeboarding, ziplining, skating, parkour, skateboarding, diving, trail running, kayaking/rafting, and cycling.

The sensations of wind in your hair, and the sun warming your heart, could be the fastest way to feel free. Play so hard and loud that you actually reach a slow motion deep silence. Savor the sensations.

Sleep is when our soul refreshes our body.

Deepak Chopra

Which part of the day are you most awake?

Sleep surely is important, since we spend 1/3 of our lives doing it. Did you know that the brain, the internet, and the universe all have similar network structures?

Our brain is definitely not passive when we are asleep; it is very active. Some believe the function of sleep is to learn from the day. Others believe it is a time to connect to all that is one, on a universal and molecular level. Some ancient civilizations believed sleep is where past, present, and future could all coincide. Whatever is going on during sleep, it is powerful.

Listen if your eyelids are heavy and complain. You may need more sleep at night to refresh your brain. Brought to you by the easier school day campaign.

The more you know the less you need.

Yvon Chouinard

----- ----- -----

When you make an activity out of simple pleasures, do they become grand adventures?

Big list of simple pleasures to do outside:

- Make a tiny boat out of a leaf.
- Press flowers in a book.
- Find the Big Dipper.
- Roll down a hill.
- Splash in puddles.
- Build a snow or branch cave.
- Eat an apple right from the tree.
- Wade in a stream.
- Make a musical instrument from nature.
- Collect 5 different kinds of rocks.
- Whittle a stick.
- Find shapes in the clouds.
- Play freeze tag in the moonlight.
- Hear your own echo.
- Climb a tree.
- Dance in the rain.
- Catch a shooting star.

Bring it back to basics.
Chat with your simple curiosities.

The mountains are calling and I must go.

John Muir

Do you have a favorite view of nature on your way to school?

A scientist used a tool, an EEG, to measure alpha waves in people. Alpha waves notice serotonin in folks. Serotonin is the neurotransmitter in the brain that fights off depression. The scientist wanted to know why sometimes people drive longer roads just to see more trees and fewer buildings.

Natural scenes, even if viewed from the car or in a picture on the wall, increased alpha waves in people. Both the pictures and the views helped to resist anxiety, anger, and aggression. That's just from looking at nature from a distance. Imagine the health benefits from actually being in a natural environment or next to a plant. The relaxation you feel doesn't need to be explained.

The science shows that we need to be outdoors way more hours than we currently are. We grow better outside.

Don't shrink, don't puff up.
Stand your sacred
ground.

Brené Brown

What if we could defeat
our deepest fears
by winning a staring
contest in the mirror?

Maybe you have noticed in movies like *The Lion King, Harry Potter, Spider Man, Wizard of Oz, Star Wars,* or *A Wrinkle in Time* - the biggest challenge is to overcome the doubts and fears inside the hero's own mind.

When standing face-to-face with the villain or problem, the character realizes that they are really confronting their internal doubts, first and foremost. The opponent was not as strong as they thought they were, and it took this voyage to discover their own path to self-confidence, self-love, and worthiness.

The fact that we get scared usually means that we are about to do something really brave. Act when you feel powerful. Get nervous later. Hold your head high and your standards higher.

You have the power to change your brain. All you have to do is lace up your running shoes.

John Ratey

How quickly can you change from tired to inspired?

Easy ways to boost your energy in 10 minutes:

1. Walk around the school. Just that little bit of endorphin boost will improve memory, mood, productivity, and focus.
2. Drink water. When we lose 1-3% of our fluids we lose motivation and feel low.
3. Take a tech break. A few minutes away actually makes a difference.
4. Get some sunshine. Vitamin D improves mood, aches, pains, and fights diseases.
5. Eat more mini-meals. Recharge with smaller bites throughout the day.
6. Smell some essential oils like peppermint.
7. Take some mindful deep breaths and do some stretching.
8. Break out the joke book. A few good laughs will raise your frequency.
9. Play and play some more. Silly actually spreads kinetic energy.

You are just one intentional move away from a better mood.

The time is always ripe to do what is right.

Martin Luther King Jr.

Do people compliment you on your integrity?

10 things people do to show leadership and others take notice:

1. Being on time
2. Showing effort
3. Working hard and focusing
4. Having positive body language
5. Bringing energy to projects
6. Having an authentic happy attitude
7. Speaking with passion
8. Being coachable
9. Asking the phrase, "how can I help?"
10. Being prepared.

You are noticed, you are valued, you are going to make a huge difference. Continue on the path of integrity and the right way will unfold for you.

The time is now.
Stop hitting the snooze
button on your life.

Mel Robbins

What if all you need is
to regularly countdown
to action? 5,4,3,2,1

Some think you one day wake up with motivation. What if it really isn't like that? What if you have to physically make yourself do the uncomfortable things?

Example: speaking up in class. When a good idea comes into your mind in class, but it may be a little scary to speak up, count down in your head 5,4,3,2,1 and just raise your hand. Chances are that it is a good idea. If it's not, so what? There's another one around the bend. Just keep exercising the courage muscles and the brain will feel easier communicating the ideas. Practice moving forward.

Another example: Doing the annoying thing at home that makes sense to do but isn't that much fun. 5,4,3,2,1 and just see what you can do in 5 minutes. Likely you made it worse in your head. Excuses are a time thief. Redesign your mind.

Where there is no struggle, there is no strength.

Oprah Winfrey

If it took hard work to learn it, does it feel more like you earned it?

A few folks who kept believing through struggle:

- Michael Jordan was cut from his high school basketball team for lack of skill.
- Einstein didn't speak until he was 4 years old. Many of the adults in his life deemed him "mentally slow".
- Abraham Lincoln failed campaigning 7 times before becoming President.
- Walt Disney was fired from a newspaper for lacking imagination and not having original ideas.
- Oprah Winfrey was demoted from her job as a news anchor because they said she wasn't fit for TV.
- The Beatles were rejected by a recording studio and told they didn't belong in show business.
- 300 business people rejected Pandora
- 51 unsuccessful games were produced before Rovio developed Angry Birds.

It goes to show, hard work and determination are needed in this world. Keep going through the struggle. Stay true to your dreams.

Actions speak louder
than words.

What's your next
exciting pursuit?

<u>A poem for inspiration:</u>
We are all going somewhere,
don't you know,
up or down, fast or slow.
We like to think we got a destination,
and we get there before our expiration.
But we got to move.
We got to go.
Got to take our place
in this crazy show.
Just sitting around gonna do no good.
Gotta jump on in like a Robin Hood.

You can curse the darkness
or curse the light.
Whatever jives with your appetite.
But the truth of it is, we got it all.
The warmth of spring, the chill of fall.
It's about the journey and not the season.
It's about the faith and not the reason.
We gonna give it our all or let it go.
Either better world or status quo.

-Howard Hanger

Let food be your medicine.

Vani Hari

- - - - -

- - - - -

- - - - -

How many health benefits can you think of for simply eating kale?

5 health benefits of kale:

1) It is one of the most nutrient-
dense foods on the planet.
2) It boosts circulation, which helps organs.
3) Kale is a rich source of vitamin C,
which keeps us from getting sick.
4) It is also a rich source of vitamin A
through beta-carotene, which
helps with strong eyesight.
5) Kale is a great anti-inflammatory so your
sore muscles and bruises go away faster.
Fewer injuries, more playing.

These are just a few of the
health benefits of kale.
Food is energy, and energy is everything.
Be the energy you want to attract.

People will forget what you said, people will forget what you did, but people will never forget how you made them feel.

Maya Angelou

How do you want to be remembered?

Silence is full of answers. Today's wisdom comes from within.

For 15 seconds, try to breathe deeply and visualize how you want others to feel about their relationship with you. Our moment of silence starts now...

<note to reader: after 15 silent seconds...softly talk again>

Breathe deeply.
And so it begins.
And so it is.

If knowledge is power, then learning is a superpower.

Jim Kwik

Do you know about neuroplasticity?

A famous learning expert was once told he was the "kid with the broken brain" by an adult in his life. It took him years and years to realize that brain cells can regenerate and he could turn his disability around. How often do we wish we didn't listen to someone's insult and waste years of believing a bad comment or opinion?

As a college student, he taught himself how to learn. He could teach himself difficult subjects, even though he had a head injury and struggled through many subjects in school.

The term neuroplasticity is one that needs to be talked about in school. We have the ability to change and shape our brains. "Neuro" is for the nerve cells, or neurons, and "plastic" refers to the changing ability of our brain and nervous system. Learning is not a spectator sport. Be the boss of your own brain.

There are no short and easy paths to long and lasting happiness.

Nick Vujicic

Have you thought about the steady and trustworthy job your heart performs?

Nick Vujicic (pronounced VOO-yee-cheech) was born without arms and legs. Throughout his childhood, Nick not only dealt with the typical challenges of school and adolescence, but he also struggled with depression and loneliness. Nick constantly wondered why he was different than all the other kids.

With deep self-reflection he started to understand that a person's heart and spirit is what counts. The path to happiness is from our mindset. He turned his life into a passionate mission to reach others who also might feel like outsiders.

Nick is now a motivational speaker teaching folks to focus on blessings, not the disabilities, we have in our lives. Who do we have in our lives that might want to have an open discussion around abilities? Grow through what you go through, together. We are made to connect.

You cannot share what
you do not have.
If you do not love
yourself, you cannot love
anyone else either.

don Miguel Ruiz

How do you take time for
solitude and reflection?

There is a very special philosophy
called The Four Agreements
by don Miguel Ruiz.

When you are able to study them
and apply them to your life, you will
likely find tremendous peace.

<u>Here are the basics:</u>
1) Be impeccable with your word.
This means say only what you
mean, and use words wisely.
2) Don't take anything personally.
What others say or do is not about you.
It's about them.
3) Don't make assumptions.
Find the courage to ask questions
and get clarity. Avoid drama.
4) Always do your best.
Your best will change from moment
to moment. When you're able, go
big. When you're not, ease up.
Simply do your best.

Love is the energy of the soul.

Gary Zukav

Do you treat love as a noun or a verb?

We are warm-blooded mammals with great intelligence. Other mammals are also very smart like dolphins, elephants, chimpanzees, and dogs. We have similar ways of taking care of our babies and showing love. That said, human beings spend the longest time taking care of their children.

This leads us to believe that one reason we have emerged into the highest ranking mammal is our commitment to love. Connecting with others in kind and supportive ways releases happy chemicals of serotonin and oxytocin. These neurotransmitters help us feel significant and trusted in friendships and teacher/student relationships.

Everyone in the school wins when folks are kind and caring. Let your heart lead the way and the school culture can change from less work to more play.

Let food be your medicine.

Vani Hari

How many health benefits can you think of for simply eating cucumbers?

<u>5 benefits of the cucumber:</u>
1) They speed up the detox process of getting rid of toxins from your body.
2) Cucumbers are a high source of ascorbic acid which helps build ligaments, tendons, and cartilage. Fewer injuries, more playing.
3) They are good for your eye health.
4) Cucumbers build collagen which helps skin repair and bounce back from cuts.
5) They lower the pressure in the arteries and help keep them hydrated.

Those are just a few of the health benefits of a cucumber.
Food is energy, and energy is everything.
Be the energy you want to attract.

The universe has shaken you to awaken you.

Gabby Bernstein

Are you listening, even when it's quiet?

"The atoms of our bodies are traceable to stars that manufactured them in their cores and exploded these enriched ingredients across our galaxy, billions of years ago. For this reason, we are biologically connected to every other living thing in the world. We are chemically connected to all molecules on Earth. And we are atomically connected to all atoms in the universe. We are not figuratively, but literally stardust."

Neil deGrasse Tyson

We hope you will take time over the break to learn more about yourself, your people, your planet and beyond.

Leave some room for stillness and mystery. Stay curious.

WISE FROM WITHIN